T0113700

THE FOREST MUST SCREAM

The Forest Must Scream
Comedy in Four Acts

Henri Djombo & Osée Colins Koagne
Translated from the French by Nsah Mala

Spears Books

Denver, Colorado

Spears Books
An Imprint of Spears Media Press LLC
7830 W. Alameda Ave, Suite 103-247
Denver, CO 80226
United States of America

First English edition published in the United States of America in 2022 by Spears
Books
www.spearsmedia.com
info@spearsmedia.com
@spearsbooks

Information on this title: www.spearsmedia.com/the-forest-must-scream
© 2022 Henri Djombo & Osée Colins Koagne, Nsah Mala
All rights reserved.

First French edition published in 2012; revised French edition co-published in
2015 by Éditions LC and Éditions Hémar.

ISBN: 9781942876922 (Paperback)
Also available in Kindle format

Cover designed by Doh Kambem
Designed and typeset by Spears Media Press LLC

Distributed globally by African Books Collective (ABC)
www.africanbookscollective.com

CONTENT

DRAMATIS PERSONNAE

KAMONA: Chief of Mbala Village
MAMIE: Chief Kamona's Wife
TAMBOU: Woodcutter, Chief Kamona's Confident
FUNCTIONARY: Forestry Guard, then Chief of the Big Village
TEACHER: Primary School Teacher
TOUBILI: Chief Kamona's Nephew
INHABITANTS OF MBALA
WOODCUTTERS
INHABITANTS OF THE BIG VILLAGE

ACT I

Chief's Palace in Mbala village.

As the curtain is raised, a light illuminates the chief's court-
yard where there is the throne and two seats, one reserved for
a visitor and another reserved for Kamona's wife. The garden
side has the sacred tree and the courtyard side has two big
trunks of wood. Woodcutters sit on these trunks during village
council meetings. There are axes and an engine saw placed on
the trunks.

SCENE 1
TAMBOU, A VILLAGER

TAMBOU
(*He enters, followed by the villager; he draws the latter's attention,*
using his fingers, to the jumbled bundles of wood under the sacred
tree.) Do you see? All this wood is only for the Chief and his family.
We are going to sell it, and as always, he will keep the revenue,
for himself, his wife and his children. He will say: "Sell this wood
for the best price and do not subtract any coin. Be careful, I will
verify to the least cent possible." I asked him if there was a vehicle
to transport all this wood, because I will not be able to do it with a
wheelbarrow, with only my two arms. And he said to me without
warning: "Are you a woman, Tambou? Have you ever seen a man
with more than two arms? Is this wood really a big task for somebody like you? Come on, go and see the customers, lazy man!"
He started shouting at me like a beast, and I ended up accepting
to transport the wood in a wheelbarrow.

THE VILLAGER
The Chief exaggerates. At this pace, he will exterminate the forest,

and what will we survive on afterwards?

TAMBOU

Until when shall we continue to follow him in this obscure business like slaves? Oh, it should not continue like this! They say that in some other quarters the chiefs are generous. Kamona will push us to quit Mbala one day, then we will go and taste goodness elsewhere. I can't stop thinking about this.

THE VILLAGER

It's true, but where will we go and hide without him unearthing and … us (*passes the sharp edge of his hand under his chin to better express the action of killing*)?

TAMBOU

Silence, he is coming.

❖ ❖ ❖

SCENE 2
TAMBOU, VILLAGER, KAMONA

KAMONA

(*Entering*) What are you still doing here? You should already be in the market, customers are waiting for you there since… Go away!

TAMBOU

Yes, Chief, I am going there right away (*starting to go out*).

KAMONA

You will buy a few things for my wife, but do not spend my money! (*Speaking to the Villager*) And you, why are you looking at me in this manner? Is your photo pasted on my forehead? (*The Villager goes out; left alone, Kamona sits on his throne; shortly afterwards he falls deeply asleep and starts mumbling.*) Ten thousand dollars, fifteen bundles…

SCENE 3
KAMONA, MAMIE, TAMBOU

MAMIE

(*Entering and surprised to find Kamona asleep*) - Haaaaaa, my husband, even in your sleep you talk about money and wood? (*She looks up to the sky, and then looks at her husband*) How can you sleep right up to this hour? It's already deep in the afternoon!

KAMONA

(*Suddenly waking up*) - Is that so! (*He removes his pipe and, noticing that he no longer has tobacco, scolds in anger.*) Where is that Tambou wasting time? Hasn't he returned from the sale of wood?

MAMIE

My husband, do not get angry! Wood sells poorly these days. We are no longer the only people in the place. Woodcutters are becoming more and more numerous. What do we do when the majority of the people are engaged in the wood business?

KAMONA

If others sell their wood, why should we not sell ours? There are trees and they will never finish. Where is that lazy Tambou wasting time?

MAMIE

Tambou is coming. We are talking about him, and there he suddenly appears.

KAMONA

At last, you are here! I was already losing patience. But (*glancing to the left and then to the right*) I do not see the money. Where is it?

TAMBOU

(*Emptying his pockets*) Here it is, Chief. After selling everything, I arranged for a lorry to transport the wood that has been cut and piled for over a month. The transporter has accepted to be paid after delivering the wood in warehouses. (*He tries to remove the remaining money in his pocket*).

KAMONA

You understand it at least, Tambou, paying in installments is not a problem for me; it is good that he has not overused my money. You can keep them, those coins, and buy cassava for your children. You are a brave boy, always deserving my confidence.

TAMBOU

(*Remembering*) Chief, I almost forgot. While coming back, I saw a very important man at the big crossroads; he was wearing a uniform as green as our forest and was speaking with the inhabitants of the neighbouring village on the subject of trees. It seemed he was saying that it is important to plant and not to cut trees!

KAMONA

Not cutting trees, but planting trees? Who would say such a stupidity, if it is not you inventing it? What is the name of that distinguished man?

TAMBOU

I don't know, Chief. People were saying that he is the new functionary in charge of Water and Forestry. As I was passing there and the people knew that I am from Mbala, they told me that he will soon arrive in our village.

KAMONA

Is he not the one in charge of organising woodcutters? Is he not the one who distributes machetes, axes, chainsaws, mobile saws and other tools for woodwork? Beat the drum to convene our population to the palace. I am waiting impatiently for the functionary; he is coming, without any doubt, to help the village. Tell the population to clean the courtyard and to go and change their clothes before his arrival! (*Tambou exits*)

SCENE 4
KAMONA, MAMIE

MAMIE

(*Pleading*) My husband, do not forget the money for the fish which I took on credit and which we ate yesterday.

KAMONA

(*Irritated*) All this because you've seen money! How much was it?

MAMIE

Ten dollars.

KAMONA

(*Ironically*) Ten dollars (*He pastes a one dollar banknote on her forehead*), I will pay the rest next time. Clean the courtyard and put on feasting clothes; we will soon receive the big functionary.

❖ ❖ ❖

SCENE 5
THE SAME, PLUS VILLAGERS, TEACHER AND TOUBILI

VILLAGERS

(*Entering one after the other and greeting one another*) Greetings, Chief! Greetings, Chief! (*Women sit on the tree trunks on the courtyard side and men stand up behind them*).

KAMONA

(*With joy*) Has everybody answered the call?

VILLAGERS

(*In chorus*) Yes, Chief.

KAMONA

(*Visibly satisfied*) It's good. Listen! Tambou has just told me that in a few hours or even minutes, a great guest will arrive in our beautiful village.

VILLAGERS

Heey! A great guest?

KAMONA

That's it. A functionary in charge of organising woodcutters is coming to visit us.

A VILLAGER

A functionary! And I thought that it was the sub-prefect! (*Mocking laughter*)

A SECOND VILLAGER

And me, I thought he was the prefect or the president of the Republic! (*Mocking laughter*)

KAMONA

(*Irritated*) Calm down yourselves, bunch of agitators! Functionaries deserve respect. We must reserve for the stranger a welcome that is worthy of Mbala. You must rehearse your dancing steps.

TAMBOU

Oh, I see a stranger coming, that may be him. Look over there!

KAMONA

No doubt, it is the big functionary! Let the dance begin! (*Villagers get up and dance around in a circle as the village chief welcomes the visitor*)

❖ ❖ ❖

SCENE 6
THE SAME, FUNCTIONARY, TOUBILI

FUNCTIONARY
(*Entering, going towards Kamona and extending his hand to greet him*) Are you really the chief of this village?

KAMONA
(*Going towards the Functionary and shaking his hand*) It's really the chief in person, is that not obvious? Welcome to Mbala, Sir. Mr agent, when a stranger arrives in Mbala, we honour him and offer him the priciest of our drinks, palm wine. Let someone immediately bring palm wine to our guest, and the priciest fruits of our land!

FUNCTIONARY
(*Drinking the wine and clicking his tongue*) What a delicious drink! Why don't lemonade breweries and factories produce it?

VILLAGERS
(*Acquiescing*) Heey!

FUNCTIONARY
Why don't they put it in bottles to commercialise it in the big cities of the world?

VILLAGERS
Well spoken! You are really a great man. (*Acclamations*)

KAMONA
(*With joy*) Mamie, give the Functionary five litres of wine! (*Mamie gets up and goes to get wine and local fruits for the Functionary*) Also take these fruits, they are the best of the land!

FUNCTIONARY
Thank you very much, I will drink this wine with great pleasure.

Let us now get to the purpose of my visit. Mr Village Chief and dear inhabitants, I thank you for the warm welcome you have just offered to me.

KAMONA

It's normal, we owe our tradition of hospitality to our ancestors. Once more, you are welcome to Mbala.

FUNCTIONARY

I am the new chief of post in charge of Water and Forestry. I have just succeeded a colleague who had, through carelessness, thrown a cigarette butt on the ground. The butt burnt a whole forest. Of course, this colleague was dismissed from his duties.

TAMBOU

Well done for him, Chief. He was very wicked towards Mbala woodcutters.

FUNCTIONARY

Today I am starting the campaign for the dissemination of the forestry code in your village. This campaign aims to sensitise the populations on the preservation of forests. The forests you are exploiting today must also serve future generations. (*Applause*)

KAMONA

(*Turning towards the functionary*) Me, I am called Chief Kamona, thirty-third descendant of the Mbala dynasty.

A VILLAGER

(*Speaking with enthusiasm to his fellow villagers while the chief makes a joke on his guest's ear*)
Finally, they will offer us these tools that we were awaiting for a long time. We will henceforth be able to cut trees and saw wood without difficulty; we will improve our living conditions. This Functionary is a great man. (*Applause*)

KAMONA

Mr Chief of Post, we are good citizens, we respect the law, we will respect the forestry code.

FUNCTIONARY

(*With satisfaction*) Mr Kamona, I congratulate you on your sense of responsibility. Where chiefs are incapable, it is not surprising that their cities resemble jungles. By the way, don't we say that a fish always starts to rot from the head? Population of Mbala, applaud your leader! (*Intense ovation*)

KAMONA

(*Very flattered, he holds his guest by the hand and leads him under the sacred tree to honour him*) Receive the blessings of our ancestors! You are here at home, I suppose that you did not cross two rivers and climbed mountains for nothing! Continue with your speech, Sir.

FUNCTIONARY

Now, I will read a very important article. It is article 144 of the forestry code.

KAMONA

We will respect article 144 of the forestry code to the last word. Long live article 144 of the forestry code! (*Applause*)

FUNCTIONARY

This article stipulates: "Any person caught in the forest without fulfilling the legal conditions for the exploitation of wood, starting bushfires or poaching wild animals…"

TAMBOU

It is what we do every day. It is our profession, Sir.

FUNCTIONARY

"This person will pay a fine ranging from one thousand to ten thousand dollars and will be subject to a prison term of at least one year…

VILLAGERS

(*In chorus*) - What!!! It is not possible. (*They mumble words and proffer curses in their language.*) Chief, do something, otherwise we are finished.

KAMONA

I will then tell him the truth!

VILLAGERS

(*In chorus*) Tell him the truth, Chief. The whole truth! Nothing but the truth!

KAMONA

This forest that you see here and around is our own heritage. Our ancestors exploited it, our fathers too. Today, we are exploiting it and tomorrow our children will exploit it, and so forth, from generation…

VILLAGERS

…to generation!

KAMONA

(*Nervous*) - It is not a small functionary like you who will come and stop us from cutting wood in this forest. We are the owners of our lands. If you are the one who planted the Mbala forest which you want to prohibit us from exploiting, remove it from here!

VILLAGERS

(*Supporting their chief*) Well spoken, Chief!

TAMBOU

(*With enchantment*) The charismatic Kamona!

FUNCTIONARY

(*Trying to calm down the chief*) Be calm! Maybe I have not made myself well understood. Like me, other agents are crisscrossing the country to sensitise the populations on the sustainable management of forests. It is the role of village chiefs, as the first authorities incarnating State power in their localities, to facilitate the task of sensitisers and take over the government campaign.

KAMONA

No! This is enough!

TAMBOU

(*With enchantment*) The charismatic!

FUNCTIONARY

Mr Kamona, you must not be carried away in this manner, you should show a good example! To be honest, after the sub-prefect, you are the first administrator of the village. That is why I invite you to personally pull yourself together, to show proof of responsibility and control your population.

KAMONA

Finally you are recognising my authority and my power! The government has just done it, by finally remunerating village chiefs for the work they accomplish daily. But how much and when did they pay us? You seem to open your eyes widely as if you are not aware that, for ages, we were the only abandoned administrators. Do you now understand how we were made to work without payment? (*Villagers applaud warmly*) And you, could you work without remuneration? Can a poor person manage a kingdom with dignity?

TAMBOU

(*With enchantment*) The charismatic! (*In anger*) By the way, great powers in the world, who use the poor to elevate themselves, would not reign if they ran out of wealth.

KAMONA

(*Trying to relieve the tense atmosphere*) We derive our wealth from our forest. Where is the problem? (*Heavy applause*)

TAMBOU

(*With enchantment*) The charismatic!

FUNCTIONARY

(*A bit out of himself*) Exactly, there would be no problems if you respected the legal conditions for wood exploitation. The State does not prohibit the cutting of firewood for your domestic needs, such as cooking, heating and lighting. On the contrary, the State does not authorise cutting enormous quantities with which you flood markets in the towns. By cutting trees so carelessly, you're causing the exhaustion of forest resources. Have you forgotten that in the past, large expanses of forests extended out of sight in this region? They have been transformed, within a short time, into simple scraps of greenery. If you do not take care, these scraps of greenery will disappear definitively. Even wildlife, which was abundant and varied, has become rare, to the point where your children will only know it through images. What a pity!

KAMONA

We have been woodcutters for generations. How are we going to live without cutting or selling wood?

FUNCTIONARY

Reflect a bit! You continue to cut wood and burn entire expanses of forests and savannas, without bothering to replace the lost trees. If your forests disappear today, your children and your grandchildren will not be able to satisfy their needs for wood tomorrow. You cannot live decently thanks to your forests if you don't respect the rules of good management.

TOUBILI

(*Detaching himself from the group*) By the way, Mr Agent, only a few skeletal trees are still standing up. (*Turning towards the functionary*) All of them will soon disappear… (*Speaking to chief Kamona*) Uncle, according to me, the Functionary is completely right. I will study, me too, to become a water and forestry agent. (*Brouhaha of discontentment*)

KAMONA
Be quiet! Who brought my nephew to this assembly for him to interfere in adult conversations? This is not a gathering for high school children! He should be sent away from here immediately! (*Toubili exits*)

FUNCTIONARY
You are wrong not to listen to the innocent voice of this child and not to follow what he is saying. However, this voice should instead inspire wisdom in you. After exhausting the best trees, now you are targeting forests on hills and mountains. No longer absorbed by the soil, water flows everywhere, on high speed, digging deep ravines, destroying roads and bridges. That is happening wherever deforestation has exceeded sustainable limits. Have you never seen houses in this village carried away into the abyss?

MAMIE
It is the work of wizards. (*She exits, annoyed*)

FUNCTIONARY
You find scapegoats in order to console yourselves. You find wizards everywhere, while you are the gravediggers.

TAMBOU
(*Furious*) Sacrilege! What? That we are gravediggers?

KAMONA
(*Unable to hide his anger*) Tell me, who can reproach the waters of a river for flowing in the direction they have chosen? You have just exceeded tolerable limits! A snake can run well, but it can

never overtake its own head. As long as I remain the chief of this
village, I have said we are going to…

VILLAGERS
(*In chorus*) … to cut!

FUNCTIONARY
You are warned. Don't try again to exploit the forests in such an
anarchic manner! On the contrary, I will prove to you that, in our
country, the State is not dead!

KAMONA
He thinks he is intimidating us. Mr Agent, I will tell you the truth:
my thirty seasons of reign at the helm of this village have immu-
nised me against exterior interference in the affairs of Mbala. My
word will not change!

TAMBOU
If you have missed the door, then go and knock elsewhere!

VILLAGERS
Never here!

KAMONA
As long as I remain chief in this village, I have said that we are
going to…

VILLAGERS
(*In anger and in chorus*)… cut!

KAMONA
(*Furious and provocative*) Cut…

VILLAGERS
(*In anger and in chorus*) … trees!

KAMONA

(*Still furious and provocative*) Right down to the roots!

TAMBOU

(*With enchantment*) The charismatic!

FUNCTIONARY

(*With despair but determined*) Alright! Whoever plants deforestation harvests drought! I will not let you do it. As a State agent, I
will make sure that the forestry code is respected everywhere, for
the good of humanity.

KAMONA

Humanity ... humanity! Is it that your humanity that feeds our
families? We are tired of words. Now is time for action. Give us
money in exchange for your demands. In any case, the forest will
serve our own development.

VILLAGERS

(*In anger and in chorus*) Our development! Go away!

FUNCTIONARY

(*Trying to calm the tension*) Mr Village Chief, the international
community is putting in place compensation mechanisms. You
will then see that owning forests offers unprecedented advantages
for the future.

KAMONA

What are these advantages?

FUNCTIONARY

These advantages are numerous: tourists will arrive here in Mbala
to visit your forests. You will sell art objects to them, you will serve
as guides to them, you will lodge and feed them. For all these
services, you will receive a lot of money. Social actions and other
advantages will add onto that to improve life for you...

KAMONA

Nonsense! Do you really believe that? It's a bluff, all of that!

FUNCTIONARY

When the time comes, you may risk regretting having destroyed your forests. Reflect a bit!

KAMONA

(*Flattered*) Reflect again on what? These famous advantages do not concern us, keep them for yourself. Every time, compensation, compensation. Who will they compensate?

TAMBOU

(*With enchantment*) The charismatic!

FUNCTIONARY

As you must know, these mechanisms are actually the object of negotiations between States, so that industries from the North should pay carbon credits to finance activities which enable the reduction of greenhouse gases elsewhere. It is the principle of the polluter payer, as we call it in our jargon!

TEACHER

What is the use of credits that we have never seen and which we shall never see? Tell us how poor villagers will have access to the credits.

FUNCTIONARY

Here, for example, in order to benefit from this funding, we must first impose a strict management of our forest resources. Moreover, we must start restoring degraded forests and planting many trees.

KAMONA

(*Curious*) You talked about green...what gases?

TAMBOU

Greenhouse gases! As in a dance in a cramped house where some greenish gases hold us together, Chief!

KAMONA

Greenhouse gases! What then are these gases? All this is not clear in our eyes!

FUNCTIONARY

(*Trying to look reassuring*) Gentlemen, they are gases found in the air. They are gases such as carbon dioxide, methane, and others which have the property to heat when they come in contact with infrared rays from the sun. Their accumulation in the atmosphere ends up elevating ambient temperatures. It is what we observe in a closed vehicle under the sun...

KAMONA

Is air itself no longer a gas?

FUNCTIONARY

Yes, air is a gas; it is even a mix of gases...

KAMONA

(*Proud and happy in front of his subjects*) It is a debate for intellectuals, my population has nothing to do with it. Let us come back to our topic. (*Loud applause*)

TAMBOU

(*With enchantment*) The charismatic! (*Intoning praises for chief Kamona*) ... He who would equal chief Kamona, thirty-third descendant of the valiant dynasty of Mbala, by intelligence, wisdom, wealth, cattle and harvests, is not yet born. He will never be born...Who is known in this countryside, in our nation and in the entire world like Kamona? (*Drums rhyme with poetry and praises until when the chief himself interrupts the music with an authoritative gesture*)

KAMONA

You have said that the populations would receive money from industries? Where is the share for Mbala? Inhabitants of Mbala, have you ever seen the colour of the money that they owe us?

VILLAGERS

(*In anger*) No! Never seen its colour!

FUNCTIONARY

These foreign industries are not yet paying the money to anybody, they will certainly do it in the future.

KAMONA

In the future, but which future again? Are we not already in the future ever since they began talking about it? In all meetings, you talk about the future. Future, future! In conferences...

VILLAGERS

... the future!

KAMONA

In congresses....

VILLAGERS

... the future!

KAMONA

In symposia....

VILLAGERS

... the future!

KAMONA

(*Taking his subjects as witnesses*) You see, there are too many futures! (*Turning towards the Functionary*) Where is the true future in all of these?

TAMBOU

The charismatic!

TEACHER

(*Coming out from his reserve*) I appreciate the attitude of the inhabitants of Mbala, especially the combative nature of their chief. Mr Agent, understand the legitimacy of their demands. Industrialised countries are asking the poor to stop cutting wood from their forests. But what will these woodcutters receive in exchange in order to survive? (*Applause*) Today, with which money can peasants be able to maintain their forests as gardens for Europe and America? Who will give them credit for that? And if there was credit, would those industries pay the debts they would have contracted tomorrow?

KAMONA

Frankly, these industries are taking us for idiots; they are mocking us! (*Heavy applause from the inhabitants who once more salute the proven intelligence and the courage of their chief*)

TAMBOU

(*With enchantment*) The charismatic!

FUNCTIONARY

(*Looking annoyed*) You are asking me too many questions, as if I am sitting on the accusation bench. Do you think I eat on the table of the polluters? I am just doing my job!

KAMONA

(*Disdainful*) Which job? Nonsense!

FUNCTIONARY

(*Revolted*) And you, Mr Teacher, instead of cornering me in this way, you should explain to these people, in simple language, the message of the government.

TEACHER

(*Indifferent*) It is legitimate, you are doing your job, the inhabitants of Mbala are doing theirs.

FUNCTIONARY

Is that so? Do you know, Sir, the price to pay for restoring a destroyed or degraded forest? That costs a lot and our government does not have the means. It is therefore better to prevent than to cure. Try to make them understand.

TAMBOU

Mr Agent, you will not get away with this!

KAMONA

Now you are seeking the understanding and complicity of a functionary like you. But, what you ignore, Sir, is that the teacher lives with us, he knows and shares in our daily sufferings.

TAMBOU

When the State deprives him of his salary or transfers it late, it is the village that feeds him. He has become an inhabitant of Mbala and will not follow somebody like you, disconnected from the realities of the countryside.

TEACHER

You have also said that these industries will never stop polluting the atmosphere because they would be paying money. To whom are they paying this money? So air will always be polluted; polluters will continue to heat and poison the earth at the detriment of the poor people of the world who do not know any saint to turn to. It is unjust!

VILLAGERS

(*In chorus*) It is unjust!

TEACHER

(*To the Functionary*) Like me, you know that the money promised, which might never come, is a poisoned gift for all of humanity, as long as manufacturers will not cease to be reluctant. As long as they do not engage definitively on quantifiable and verifiable objectives for the reduction of their greenhouse gases. Before asking poor woodcutters for their part of the effort, it is first important for industries to stop polluting and that they fulfil their financial obligations towards the former.

TAMBOU

By the way, nobody knows anything yet about their intentions.

KAMONA

Good! What can we understand from the vagueness of this situation? I repeat: Pay the money that we need in order to ameliorate our living conditions and we will spare the forest.

TEACHER

Yes, Sir, the poor need this money in order to adapt to climate change and fight against greenhouse effects! (*Applause*)

KAMONA

(*Speaking to the Functionary*) Our population is waiting for that greenhouse effect. Let it come to Mbala, and we will prove to it that we are warriors, steeped in the traditions, throughout centuries.

FUNCTIONARY

The greenhouse effect is a reality you are already living, Sir.

KAMONA

A reality? You are uttering abstractions and babbling in order to confuse our minds. Stop treating us like this! (*To the villagers*) Inhabitants of Mbala, Mr Agent did not want to tell us that the industries that dirty the air we breathe are killing, bit by bit, all the poor people on earth. Is that normal?

VILLAGERS

(*In chorus*) No! It is unacceptable!

KAMONA

Population of Mbala, is it just for industries to continue polluting the air while we are forbidden from cutting wood?

VILLAGERS

(*In chorus*) No! We will exploit our wood!

TEACHER

Finally, these industries must help woodcutters to change their profession with clean money, that is, money that is not dirty! Moreover, why should we always borrow? And our State? What is it doing in order to enable woodcutters in Mbala and elsewhere to change their activities? (*Applause*)

KAMONA

Chief, you are right: it is by cutting wood that we will develop Mbala and will make it a beautiful town.

FUNCTIONARY

That is it, and that is also false at the same time!

KAMONA

… Do not stress yourself, Mr Agent, our decision was already taken a long time ago. I have said that we are going to…

VILLAGERS

…cut!

FUNCTIONARY

As the forestry code stipulates, the cutting of trees is only permitted for people who pay fees and respect the quantity of wood authorised by the forestry administration. Nobody is supposed to ignore the law! Nobody, in any case nobody, is above the law!

Whoever cuts trees without authorisation is exposing themselves to heavy penalties. Have all of you understood well?

KAMONA

Stranger, you do not have the right to get angry in this village nor to threaten the peaceful inhabitants of Mbala. Do you want to suffer the wrath of our ancestors? Come on, let us finish it, you will see what you will see! (*The Functionary decides to go away, but the crowd pursues him, catches him around the corner, seizes the mobile telephone he has removed from his pocket to call for help, as well as his gourd of palm wine; the crowd brings him back, his arms crossed behind his back*) Mr Agent, you have offended us right in our own village. According to our customs, we should have killed you if we weren't respecting the laws of this country. You are all alone. What do you think you can do against us? Do you know that every stranger who offends us on Mbala soil deserves a death penalty? Do you want me to order my valiant woodcutters to cut your head and turn your teeth into necklaces (*Staring in his eyes*), do you want that? You are lucky because we are good citizens. (*Speaking to Tambou*) Tambou, release him! Let him go away! (*Turning to the Functionary*) Note that this is the last time you would ever set your feet on Mbala land, the land of our ancestors. You are also seeing us for the last time. Go away! (*The Functionary escapes*)

❖ ❖ ❖

SCENE 7
KAMONA, VILLAGERS

VILLAGERS

(*In anger*) He even wanted to go with our wine and our fruits. What impertinence!

KAMONA

(*Speaking to villagers*) Well done for all you did to him, he did not deserve it. He started by speaking well; afterwards, the devil put bad words in his mouth, to the point of rendering him impolite to us. However, there is no rule without an exception. Did you not see provocation in his attitude? He is really swollen, this guy!

TAMBOU

Chief, I seized his telephone. Let us verify what he put into this device, we will know everything he has said in his communications.

KAMONA

My dear inhabitants, the entire world is plotting against this very small village. What has Mbala done for them to prohibit us from cutting wood? And that without anything in exchange! They first prohibited hunting.

VILLAGERS

… then bushfires and traps, Chief!

KAMONA

(*In anger*) Afterwards, they fell on fishing, introducing hippopotamuses and crocodiles in our rivers and streams...by transforming the whole country into protected areas. The North…

VILLAGERS

Protected zone!

KAMONA

The South…

VILLAGERS

Protected zone!

KAMONA

The East…

VILLAGERS

Protected zone!

KAMONA

The Centre…

VILLAGERS

Protected zone!

KAMONA

The West…

VILLAGERS

Protected zone! Oh! Oh! Water and Forestry!

KAMONA

And now is the turn of the forest. They want to stop us from cutting wood there!

VILLAGERS

(*In anger*) Hey!!! Even simple wood!

KAMONA

We, the woodcutters, we will send our children to school with….

VILLAGERS

(*In anger*) What?

KAMONA

(*Still in anger*) Me, I will marry my new wives with….

VILLAGERS

(*Silence*) ….

KAMONA

Me, I will have pocket money from….

VILLAGERS

What?

KAMONA

Do they want to say there will no longer be wood for woodcutters?

VILLAGER

What? No wood for woodcutters?

KAMONA

They are mistaken. Listen to me! As the chief of Mbala and the first owner of the land, I say that we are going to…

VILLAGERS

… cut!

KAMONA

We are going to…

VILLAGERS

… cut!

KAMONA

Cut…?

VILLAGERS

(*As if elated*) … trees!

KAMONA

(*Making a gesture of destruction and vengeance*) Right down to their roots!

TAMBOU

(*With enchantment*) The charismatic!

KAMONA

The forest will bleed this year. (*With determination*) Count on me, the forest will scream from pain. You will hear the screams of the forest. Dear inhabitants of Mbala, worthy woodcutters, we must increase the production of wood this year!

TAMBOU

(*With enchantment*) The charismatic!

KAMONA

Given that demand and prices have significantly increased in the market, we will double the production of wood. As the famous agent was impolite to us, take your axes, your chain saws! Enter into the forest, whether by day or by night. Whatever the name, the size or the height of a tree, cut it! Here I am the chief, have confidence in me!

TAMBOU

(*With enchantment*) The charismatic!

❖ ❖ ❖

SCENE 8
KAMONA, MAMIE, VILLAGERS

MAMIE

(*Entering with panic and holding a radio set in her hand*) My husband, I think you should listen to the radio news.

KAMONA

(*Scolds his wife*) Is it already news time?

RADIO

(*Credits on musical background*) "You are listening to Radio Giraffe, the environmental channel, the sustainable development channel, the fauna and flora channel… The council of ministers met today. It examined the only point on the agenda: wood exploitation in our country. (*A happy Kamona invites, with a hand gesture, his subjects to listen to the radio news*) The government ruled today on the control of the wood industry in our country… The fight against illegal cutting of trees must be general, it will be carried out without pity in order to eliminate bad practices which endanger ecosystems and deprive society of possibilities for development. Anybody desiring to exploit timber, must pay all their fees and pay a deposit amounting to five hundred thousand dollars into the Public Treasury. The person will respect the investment calendar and particular specifications by constructing roads, schools and dispensaries, by equipping these, by planting trees in order to reconstitute the permanent national forestry estate, by ameliorating the working conditions of employees and local populations... Some uncivic actions have been recorded in our countrysides. They will be punished in an exemplary manner. This is the case of Mbala village, whose chief has been dismissed from his duties starting from today and who must answer for his actions in competent courts..." (*Consternation in the whole village*)

KAMONA

Didn't I say it? The forestry agent has told lies about us, he has betrayed us. It is my fault. Why did I release him from your hands, at the moment when you were preparing to slaughter him? And now... (*Exasperated, he quits the scene*)

❖ ❖ ❖

SCENE 9
TAMBOU, VILLAGERS, MAMIE

MAMIE

(*Calling on the population to defend her husband's cause*) People who are warriors never accept humiliation. Mbala is humiliated; we will not betray our traditions. We must rise up like one man in order to oppose this provocation which undermines the dignity of our dynasty.

TAMBOU

(*Hypocritical*) It's a great misfortune which has befallen our village.

What! The chief dismissed? It is a plot which we must not accept. By the way, who will replace him? That is the question.

MAMIE

It's false, that is not the question! We must say NO to the government and remind them that, in our collective memory, neither dismissed chiefs nor ex-chiefs exist. A chief reigns until his death.

A VILLAGER

This is very true!

MAMIE

What a big shame for us if he is ever dragged to the courts! Could there be a traitor among us who may want to betray us and take the throne? Who is the traitor? (*Mamie sweeps the villagers in a suspicious look and quits the scene*)

VILLAGERS

(*In chorus*) Nooo! (*They disperse in groups while Chief Kamona is still locked up in his house. Some woodcutters remain near Tambou*)

❖ ❖ ❖

SCENE 10
TAMBOU, SOME WOODCUTTERS

TAMBOU

(*Seizes the opportunity to distance himself from the chief's policy on the forest exploitation*) Before tackling the question of the chief's dismissal, it is important at least to recognise that it is normal for the government to encourage massive exploitation of the forests while combating those who illegally exploit forest resources. To be honest, what do we contribute to the creation of national wealth? Almost nothing!

A WOODCUTTER

Yes, this message means that only regular actors in the sector will henceforth operate in this country, because they create jobs, pay salaries to their workers, pay fees and taxes to the State and enable the latter to function.

TAMBOU

We must however recognise that we are ravaging the forest and paying nothing into State coffers!

SECOND WOODCUTTER

The government is inviting us now to become exemplary exploiters. And see how the chief is refusing to admit it. It is him and his family who benefit from our work. What do we gain from it?

TAMBOU

Nothing, exactly! All the revenues go into their pockets! Anyway, the preservation of forestry estates is becoming an exigency and more and more serious and complex. We must change our professions, but what will we do thereafter?

THIRD WOODCUTTER

We are destroying the forest without counting. We light fires wherever we want to hunt game. To be honest, Kamona and his people have pushed too long into illegality. Now that what will happen resembles a cataclysm for our professions, what are we going to become?

TAMBOU

Presently the break is over. Deforestation is also over. We must reconvert ourselves, my friends. We are no longer executioners of orders and must henceforth speak our mind.

SECOND WOODCUTTER

Even nature is acting against us. But what are we going to do?

TAMBOU

Storms are uprooting too many trees. It is normal since the trees are isolated and therefore exposed to wind. (*He imitates the noise of wind and the falling of trees*) Without us, how are housewives going to cook food? What will become of traders, carpenters, cabinetmakers and all other professionals who depend on wood?

SECOND WOODCUTTER

As long as housewives in the city do not learn to use other sources of energy and to buy from legalised enterprises, we will remain indispensable. It is they who will come by night knocking on our doors and begging us to sell wood to them. It will therefore not be easy to eradicate the phenomenon and to blow up the actual chain.

TAMBOU

(*Ironical*) What is the State waiting for before planting baobabs in Mbala and her environs?

THIRD WOODCUTTER

What? Baobabs! What for?

TAMBOU

Since baobabs do not produce firewood, nobody will cut them, except in order to feed timber industries which will give a different face to the village.

FIRST WOODCUTTER

You are right. I think that in order to terrorise forest looters, we should introduce leopards and lions there. (*Laughter*)

TAMBOU

Let's come back to our topic. The chief is dethroned (*He attempts to sit on the chief's armchair, and is pushed away by a woodcutter*), what are we going to do? Does nature no longer hate vacancy? So, who will replace…

SCENE 11
TAMBOU, WOODCUTTERS, KAMONA

KAMONA

(*Alerted by a snitch, enters and surprises his collaborators in a meeting*) Traitors! You dare rejoice over a measure which undermines our common interests? Anyway, there is no wood again to be cut, what are we going to talk about? Look at the desert already around us… Look into my eyes! You see, it is not difficult to detect traitors among you. You are all beating eyelids in order to avoid the look of truth on my face. You are cowards, I have always known it, especially you Tambou. Nobody will replace me, note this once and for all. Nobody, I say! I will kill whoever will want to take Kamona's throne! (*He exits*)

ACT II

The scene is empty. Enter three villagers who sit in a circle, then the village Chief joins them.

SCENE 1
KAMONA, THREE VILLAGERS, MAMIE

VILLAGER
They have not produced anything, rain is still not falling!

KAMONA
(*Facing a famished and desperate population*) Oh heaven! What calamity! We have already offered sacrifices to the spirits of our ancestors...

MAMIE
(*Consoling her husband*) We will lose nothing by restarting, my husband.

KAMONA
(*Addressing Tambou with despair*) I would like to hold a meeting with the men.

TAMBOU
(*He sends out the women*) Our ancestors used to say that the surface of a lake only stirs when an object is thrown on it, or when wind blows on it! I have heard people say that, in a faraway village, a woman in anger cursed nature. The curse caused an unprecedented famine in the countryside and neighbouring lands. You have all understood...

VILLAGER

Cursed be that woman!

KAMONA

(*Relieved*) How are we going to undo this fault in order for the ancestors to forgive us? (*Drums vibrate from the four corners of the chiefdom and songs are mixed with incantations in an unknown language attributed to ancestors, it would appear, whose spirits have invaded the place. Someone announces that the village chief will make a confession. Kamona, seated on his throne, takes a position of supplication, then addresses the assembly.*) Let me be alone now. (*He is visibly desperate, and stares into space and starts to meditate aloud.*) What fault have we committed that we do not deserve forgiveness? If I had only one wife, I would have been able to feed her. If I had only two, I would have still been able. But I have so many, where do I find food in these times of drought? (*He gets up and sits down again.*) If I had only one child, I would have been able to feed him. If I had only two, that would have still been okay. But how do I feed a battalion of children? We are proud to be the descendants of people who were warriors, people who were hardworking, of these worthy people whom you have incarnated. In difficult times, we must implore your forgiveness and generosity. (*Getting up and moving towards the sacred tree to speak to ancestors.*) Proud and noble ancestors, permit me to address you in this place and at this moment in order to access your favours. You have often accomplished our wills, even if sometimes we did not deserve your confidence. You have covered us with goodness because you have always loved us; you bore our whims as prodigal children. Proud and noble ancestors, do not abandon us to our sad fate. After torrential rains as we have never seen before, gutters have been dug everywhere; they caused enormous ravines. As if that was not enough, a very severe drought lasting for months has burnt crops and decimated livestock. The little wood that we send to be sold in the city is systematically seized by the forestry police and we no longer have resources. Famine is reigning and despair has settled in our entire countryside. Desperately, days follow days and resemble themselves, without ever bringing anything to the village again, carrying away our illusions of change every time. We live like recluses who are satisfied by their own image as reflected by a deformed mirror. Time has stopped for our village. A page has been turned. Mbala is abandoned to herself. The nation has forgotten about her, because of the disobedience she manifested by abusively cutting trees, by brutalising a State agent and by opposing my dismissal from the throne. We have played with fire, it is burning us now. We are deeply sorry for that. We inherited the spirit of warriors from you, that is why dignity lives in us, so that we should not dishonour you and so that we should always face the enemy with courage. Give us rain! It will water the soil and produce a harvest; it will deliver us from pain and save your lost children. Give us your protection, so that the government should renounce the measures adopted against us! We will slaughter, at dawn, what remains for us as livestock. On your tombs, we will place victuals and palm wine in your honour. (*He empties half of his cup at the foot of the sacred tree.*) Drink, proud and noble ancestors, drink.

ACT III

The chief's palace.

SCENE 1
KAMONA, MAMIE, TOUBILI

MAMIE
(*Surprised and happy*) Toubili, Toubili, welcome back to Mbala!
You look handsome! But you have grown a lot!

TOUBILI
Thank you, my aunt. Has my uncle gone out?

MAMIE
(S*he runs and announces Toubili's return to Kamona, then comes
back*) Hold on a bit, he is coming. There he is!

KAMONA
(*Entering and visibly tired, almost desperate, but trying to be of
good humour*) Welcome back, my nephew, how was the journey?

TOUBILI
Difficult, especially when I entered Mbala land. What heat! What
matters after all, my uncle, is that I am in your midst. (*All three
of them sit down.*)

KAMONA
Toubili, you have just finished your studies. I am happy for you.
You have honoured us through your brilliant results: doctor in
ecology! It means you have really grown up, you have become a
man, a great man among us. Perhaps you would bring us a bit of
rain. For years, by the way, since you left us, it has not rained in this

village. No matter how much we offered sacrifices to the ancestors and performed rain rituals, nothing has happened.

MAMIE

The rain is angry with us, but why then?

TOUBILI

It is with good reason! One would say that a bulldozer came and destroyed all the trees which I had left green in this village, eight years ago. What happened? How, in so short a time, were you able to destroy trees right down to their roots? How were you able to exterminate wildlife to the point that your hunting rifles are no longer useful, except for settling scores over adultery? We can no longer see a rat passing by, it is a terrible catastrophe!

KAMONA

We acted out of vengeance. You do remember, a small agent of Water and Forestry…a miserable functionary tried to affront and offend us.

TOUBILI

My uncle, they say blindness and rebellions have their consequences. The most important thing is to assume them. Know that if we cut trees without replacing them, the naked soil will get poor and dry; it is then exposed to floods and erosions. Heat increases and augments drought. Know too that trees absorb carbon gases in the air and, at the same time, liberate oxygen which is indispensable for life.

MAMIE

Is that so?

TOUBILI

Yes, my aunt. Vegetation protects the soil from water runoffs, maintains humidity and facilitates evaporation, which provokes rain. It is also important to know that trees form a hedge against winds, purify the air, regulate water sources and preserve biodiversity made up of plants and animals of all types… Meanwhile, the trees which were fulfilling these functions had been cut by the inhabitants of Mbala! Today can we say where seasons for hunting big game, for harvesting mushrooms, honey, wild fruits, and for collecting caterpillars have gone to? Let's think about it! We will notice that we are only harvesting what we planted.

KAMONA

Enough! That is enough! Is that all that you went to study for many years at the university? You should have studied medicine to cure the sickness which no longer quits us… Death is watching, don't mind our appearances. The situation is more difficult than you think. Let us leave everything in the hands of the ancestors!

TOUBILI

It is still good to know, uncle. You acted out of anger and ignorance. The calamity would not have occurred if you had listened to the message of the forestry agent. Now, the desert has invaded the village and its environs. The air is too hot, polluted. Life has become unbearable. It is not the forestry agent who is suffering today, it is us! What are we going to do now?

KAMONA

We can start the rain ritual afresh…

TOUBILI

It will not change anything, uncle. Let us be honest! Let us face it and stop nursing illusions for ourselves!

KAMONA

Your position really astonishes us. You behave as if you are no longer one of us. Your opinions all seem to oppose ours, and your judgements are very severe towards your people. Is this how a good son behaves vis-à-vis his family? Toubili, do not forget particularly that you were born and bred in Mbala. Your umbilical cord was buried here, do you know it at least? It is us who sent you to school to be trained. Now our child is placing himself at the summit of the mountain to constantly teach us lessons. Would you want a curse to fall on you?

❖ ❖ ❖

SCENE 2
MAMIE, KAMONA, TOUBILI, TAMBOU, VILLAGERS

TAMBOU

(*Entering while running*) Chief, Chief, a newspaper with your photo and a letter addressed to you. They come from the sub-prefect.

KAMONA

(*With joy*) See, finally, some good news! You are the ones who underestimate me in this village. I am a popular man. The State has thought of us. Maybe the government has reconsidered her decision. Maybe she has decided to regreen our village. I accept her offered hand. Toubili, my glasses are broken, announce the good news to me by reading in my place!

TOUBILI

(*Commenting on the newspaper and letter from the sub-prefecture*) Uncle, as always, Mbala is in the bad headlines. Her inhabitants are accused. They are presented to national and international opinion as bad citizens. The sub-prefect's letter says the same thing and orders the inhabitants of Mbala to…

KAMONA

(*Suspicious*) Is all what you are saying there written near my photo?

TOUBILI

I am just translating what is written, my uncle.

KAMONA

Why translate the writings instead of simply reading them? Good, continue, in order not to waste time.

TOUBILI

The sub-prefect's letter orders the inhabitants of Mbala to quit the countryside. The reason is that you have cut trees and destroyed the forest. You have thus demonstrated a lack of patriotism, whereas, for a long time, the Water and Forestry service had warned you to stop deforestation and anarchy…

KAMONA

I still remember it myself, as if that was just yesterday.

TOUBILI

… the disappearance of the forest has led to a protracted absence of rains and a long drought in the village and its environs. Life has become impossible in the village. It is for this reason that, since yesterday, a decree of the Head of State declared a disaster in the zone… The sub-prefect's letter concludes by ordering the inhabitants of Mbala to quit as soon as possible, before the police come here to force them out.

ALL

(*Astonished*) Why?

KAMONA

We will quit this village, leaving our ancestors' tombs and charms, to go where?

TOUBILI

500 km towards the north.

KAMONA

No, I will not go there, I am going nowhere. Our ancestors are buried here and I will remain here!

TOUBILI

It is no use to continue to be stubborn to the State, it is a fight lost in advance, the police will arrive soon.

VILLAGER

Oh! Oh! The police? Things are then becoming serious. Let's go away from here!

KAMONA

(*Finally decides to go; then while hiding his tears, he collects a handful of earth at the foot of the sacred tree, contemplates it with regret and puts it in his pocket*) - Toubili, it is you who came with this misfortune in my village. Tell me: will I still be Chief where we are going?

TOUBILI

My uncle, of what use is it for a good man to bear a title if he is not up to the missions that come with it? You already have many problems. Let us go away!

KAMONA

What have they really written on this piece of paper?

TOUBILI

I have however just given you the explanation... disaster zone! (*As if under the spell of a bomb, the villagers get up, control themselves and become emotional. Then a long procession moves in the direction of the North. A funeral melody accompanies it. Children and women are crying. They walk and in front of them is the despair of a deserted horizon.*)

ACT IV

THE BIG VILLAGE

SCENE 1
KAMONA, TOUBILI, TAMBOU, FUNCTIONARY, INHABIT-
ANTS OF THE BIG VILLAGE, POET

KAMONA
What do I see from afar? Sheets covering farms?

TOUBILI
No, uncle! What we perceive there are basins which retain rain-
water and feed farms and ponds of the countryside.

TAMBOU
Oh, see this beautiful landscape, and this orchard, what a wonder!
And these varied trees lined afar like soldiers! Look at the other
side, virgin forests which remind us of our best years in Mbala.
(*The procession arrives and stops in a village bigger than Mbala.
Kamona requests hospitality.*)

POET
(*With joy*) What a melody! What enchantment! I hear music from
our home, the melody of our childhood. It is singing the freckles
of savannas which spread, out of sight, from east to west, as if
by accident, in the very middle of my country which effort and
ambition will one day place at the centre of the world. It boasts the
heights of plateaux and the reigns of mountains which audaciously
point to the sky with their stone tops, as if they were monitoring
this eternally blue expanse. What do I hear again? Yes, I hear
the voice singing, boasting of parks and natural reserves, dream
landscapes and wonderful sites, the exceptional beauty of nature,

smooth water sources which will be engulfed by the ocean, infinite beaches awaiting tourists, the vertigo of falls which cannot be found anywhere else, gorges and vestiges whose sparks illuminate the day and mystify the depth of the night, fish with fantastic names which inhabit ponds, streams, rivers, seas and oceans. Yes, I hear the voice singing our fauna, boasting the elephant, the cheetah, the gorilla, the buffalo, the antelope, the hippopotamus, and there, the pangolin, the lamantine, the crocodile, birds, these animals which live in forests, in savannas, in water, on mountains and everywhere in the universe. Yes, I have heard this voice boasting about all these riches. I have heard it sing the gift of heaven and of our ancestors, sing this heritage bequeathed by past generations, which we are obliged today to use sparingly.

FUNCTIONARY

(*Welcoming*) Thank you, Poet, for reminding us of the wonders of our nature and the duty we have to protect them. (*Then remembering*) Oh, you over there, are you not the former Chief of Mbala village?

KAMONA

Yes, it is really me, the incontestable Chief of Mbala! I have never been a former chief, that is what our traditions stipulate.

FUNCTIONARY

What has brought you to our land? You are welcome, feel at home here!

KAMONA

(*Surprised*) Oh, but are you the chief of post…?

FUNCTIONARY

I am the ex-chief of post. When they heard that you had mistaken me and threatened me with death in your village, while I was on a State mission to save forests, the inhabitants of this big village decided to place me at its helm. That was the day you missed the appointment with your future and when the heavens crashed on your heads.

KAMONA

My brother, I regret our ignorance and our behaviour towards you. When I remember that we almost killed you...oh, it's abominable! Anger is a short madness that we must be careful about. My nephew Toubili who was still a high school child at the time of the happenings understood you more than adults. He even went and studied your profession and explained everything to us upon his return. We are on our knees before you, my people and myself, and we implore your forgiveness.

FUNCTIONARY

The government informed us about your arrival in our village. (*Ironically*). Have you come to destroy the forests here?

INHABITANTS OF MBALA

(*In chorus*) No, Chief!

FUNCTIONARY

Look, forestry agents are monitoring our environs. Nobody here can behave like a vandal! Over there, farther, an acclimatation forest!

TOUBILI

Yes, I know; it facilitates the evaporation of water. The concentration of water vapour in the atmosphere forms clouds. Clouds, in turn, produce rain which mitigates drought and helps plants to grow. We can only congratulate ourselves for the harmony that reigns in this place, can't we?

KAMONA

Toubili, I have told you to leave us in peace, haven't you heard? Do you think everybody here understands the theories you are repeating over and over? You are blowing the air for us with your scholarly reasoning!

FUNCTIONARY

As if by chance, you have arrived on the day when operation "Green Country" is starting all over the national territory. Lost on the way as you were, we are not sure you know about it! The government is launching a reforestation and tree-planting programme. She wants to enlarge the permanent forest estate, enrich and preserve biodiversity, fight against drought and create decent living conditions for everyone. (*Turning towards Kamona, he emphasises to his attention*) Mr Kamona, the national police is waiting for you on the other side. You are under arrest and will be taken to court for inciting a rebellion, violation of the forestry code, blows and injuries on a State agent, damage to the integrity of nature, and many other breaches of the law. (*To the inhabitants of Mbala*) My people are ready to plant billions of trees. They are committed to follow the government in her fight. If you really want it, join her.

INHABITANTS OF MBALA

(*In chorus*) Yes, we will plant trees! (*Women and children take the lead, in a hurry to plant trees and guarantee their future. Toubili follows them, while men advance, nonchalantly towards the cleared field, all eyes looking outside to witness Kamona's arrest. On site, a gathering of youth animates the tree-planting ceremony, punctuated by an immense concert of rap music.*)

CURTAIN

ABOUT THE AUTHORS

Henri Djombo

Henri Djombo is a seasoned politician, novelist and playwright from the Republic of Congo. Djombo was born in 1952 in Enyellé village in the Likouala Region in northern Congo-Brazzaville. He holds a Master's degree in Forestry Economics from the Forestry Technology Academy in Leningrad, present-day St Petersburg, in the former USSR. Between 1980 and 2021, he served in various ministerial capacities in his native Congo, including as Minister of Water and Forests (1980-1985), Minister of Sustainable Development, Forest Economy and Environment (2009-2016), and Minister of Agriculture, Livestock and Fisheries (2016-2021). He is a member of the Political Bureau of the Congolese Labour Party (PCT) and has served four terms as a Member of Parliament. He is currently MP for the Enyellé Constituency. He has published ten novels, including *Lumières des temps perdu, Vous mourrez dans dix jours, Sur la braise, and Gahi ou l'affaire autochtone*, among others. His other plays include *Les Bénévoles* and *Le Mal de terre*. Djombo has won many literary prizes such as le Prix Amadou-Cissé-Dia du théâtre (2018), le Prix littéraire Jean-Malonga (2019), and le Prix Toussaint L'Ouverture (2019).

Osée Colins Koagne

Osée Colins Koagne is a Cameroonian stage director, playwright, and environmental theatre promoter. He was born on 14 October 1973 in Bafoussam, Cameroon. He received theatre training at the Franco-Cameroonian Alliance in Garoua, Cameroon and at the Sartrouville Theatre in Paris, France. Upon his return from France, he trained as an environmentalist under a German NGO in North Cameroon and managed the Centre for Rural Education in Ngong, about 200km from Garoua. Thanks to his activism on desertification, Koagne was invited by Sylvestre Naah Ondoa, the then Cameroon Minister of Environment and Forests, to participate in the first Conference of Ministers of Environment for the Sustainable Management of Central African Forests in Yaoundé in 2000. Thereafter, Koagne undertook an international tour to share his expertise and experience in the central African sub-region. Koagne was invited by Minister Henri Djombo to settle in Congo-Brazzaville in 2001 as a Technical Assistant at the Congolese Ministry of Forest Economy, Sustainable Development and Environment. Koagne now resides in Brazzaville and manages the *Association pour la Culture de Protection de la Faune et de la Flore* (ACPF), a pro-environment NGO.

ABOUT THE TRANSLATOR

Nsah Mala

Nsah Mala is a poet, children's author, writer, editor, translator, teacher, and literary scholar from Mbesa, Cameroon. He writes in Mbesa, English, and French. He has published five poetry collections: *Chaining Freedom, Bites of Insanity, If You Must Fall Bush, CONSTIMOCRAZY: Malafricanising Democracy*, and *Les Pleurs du mal* (French). As a writer for children, his published picture books include: *Andolo – the Talented Albino* (English), *Andolo – l'albinos talentueux* (French), *Little Gabriel Starts to Read* (English), and *Le petit Gabriel commence à lire* (French). Nsah Mala's picture book, *What the Moon Cooks,* will be published in fall 2022 by POW! Kids Books (USA). He has co-edited an international bilingual poetry anthology on the war in Anglophone Cameroon titled *Corpses of Unity - Cadavres de l'unité* (2020). He has also translated the picture book *Be a Coronavirus Fighter* (Yeehoo Press) into French as *Un Combattant du Coronavirus* (March 2020). He won the Ministry of Arts and Culture Short Story Prize (Cameroon) in 2016 and le Prix Littéraire Malraux (France) in 2017. He is an alumnus of the Caine Prize Writing Workshop.

ABOUT THE PUBLISHER

Spears Books is an independent publisher dedicated to providing innovative publication strategies with emphasis on African/Africana stories and perspectives. As a platform for alternative voices, we prioritize the accessibility and affordability of our titles in order to ensure that relevant and often marginal voices are represented at the global marketplace of ideas. Our titles – poetry, fiction, narrative nonfiction, memoirs, reference, travel writing, African languages, and young people's literature – aim to bring African worldviews closer to diverse readers. Our titles are distributed in paperback and electronic formats globally by African Books Collective.

Connect with Us: Go to www.spearsmedia.com to learn about exclusive previews and read excerpts of new books, find detailed information on our titles, authors, subject area books, and special discounts.

Subscribe to our Free Newsletter: Be amongst the first to hear about our newest publications, special discount offers, news about bestsellers, author interviews, coupons and more! Subscribe to our newsletter by visiting www.spearsmedia.com

Quantity Discounts: Spears Books are available at quantity discounts for orders of ten or more copies. Contact Spears Books at orders@spearsmedia.com.

Host a Reading Group: Learn more about how to host a reading group on our website at www.spearsmedia.com

Printed in the United States
by Baker & Taylor Publisher Services